Why can't I grow a pebble?

Because pebbles are
not living things.

Only living things
such as plants, animals
and people can grow.

Stones, metals, bricks
and plastics are not
living things.

Why are nuts so hard to open?

Because they have a tough outer shell.

Nuts are seeds. A seed contains a tiny new plant and food to help it grow.

The tough outer shell protects this plant parcel until the seed is ready to sprout.

Why can't I grow seeds in winter?

Because most seeds can't grow when it's very cold.

Seeds grow best in spring,
when the rain falls and
the sun warms the soil.
Rain makes the seeds swell.
Sunshine helps them to grow.

Why can't I have tea with my plant?

Because plants don't eat.

Plants take in food
in a different way from people.
They are the only living things
that can make their own food
inside themselves.

All they need is sunlight,
air, water and goodness
from the soil.

Why do plants need water?

Because water helps them to stay alive.

Plants soak up water
through their roots.
The water moves up
through the stem
to the leaves.

The leaves use
some of the water
for making food.

Why can't I keep my plant in the dark?

Because plants need light
to stay healthy and strong.

Plant leaves use sunlight to make food and
help them build their roots, stems and leaves.

Plants cannot
make food
if they are kept
in the dark.

They grow weak
and their leaves
turn pale.

Why can't I grow plants without soil?

Because most plants need soil to grow.

Soil holds water that the plant roots soak up. It also has goodness in it.

Plants need this goodness to grow strong and healthy.

Why can't I take my plant for a walk?

Because plants have roots that hold them firmly in the soil.

Plants don't have to search for food. They can spend their whole lives rooted in one place.

Their roots stop them from falling over or blowing away in the wind.

Why can't I push this tree over?

Because its roots are too deep, wide and strong.

Trees are the biggest plants on earth. They can grow taller than a house.

Trees have a strong woody stem, called a trunk, and deep spreading roots.

Why don't many trees have leaves in winter?

Because leaves fall off in the autumn, when the days become shorter and darker.

In the autumn, there is not enough sunlight for leaves to make food.

autumn

When the leaves can no longer work, they die and fall off.

summer

winter

spring

Then the tree rests until next spring when new leaves start growing.

Why can't I grow a pineapple in my garden?

Because pineapples can grow only in hot places.

Different plants grow in different places. Cacti grow best in dry deserts. Waterlilies grow in muddy ponds. Fir trees grow on cold mountainsides.

cacti

waterlilies

fir trees

Why can't I eat thistles?

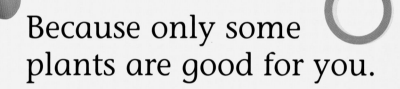

Because only some plants are good for you.

Fruit and vegetables, grains, seeds and nuts are good foods.

Thistles are too hairy and prickly to eat. Other plants are too bitter or poisonous.

Why can't I pick nettles?

Because they will sting you.

Plants cannot run away from
animals that want to eat them.

Nettles have stinging hairs
and other plants have prickles
to protect themselves.

Why can't I pick all kinds of wild flowers?

Because if everyone picked them, there would soon be none left.

Flowers make seeds,
so that new plants
can grow.
If you pick a flower,
it does not have
time to make seeds.

Without seeds,
no new flowers
can grow.

Why can't I live without plants?

Because plants give us all sorts of things we need to live.

Plants give us food such as fruit and vegetables, bread and pasta. They give us wood for buildings and fuel to keep us warm.

Plants make the air good to breathe.

Plant words

desert A very dry place where it hardly ever rains.

flower The part of a plant that turns into fruit.

fruit The part of a plant that holds seeds. People can eat sweet and juicy fruits.

leaf Plants make food in their leaves.

nut A fruit with a hard outer shell.

root Roots hold a plant firmly in the soil. They also take in water for the plant.

seed Most plants grow from seeds.

soil The earth in which plants grow.

stem The stem holds up the plant. It carries water and food to other parts of the plant.

tree A type of plant that often grows to a big size. The largest living thing on earth is a tree. Trees live longer than any other plants and some live longer than any animal.

Can you find out what these phrases mean?

- a bed of roses
- a bed of thorns
- in a nutshell
- a hard nut to crack
- pear-shaped

- to put down roots
- to shake like a leaf
- as fresh as a daisy
- to spill the beans
- to hear the grass grow

Think of another word to describe someone who is:

- weedy
- wooden
- green-fingered
- full of beans
- willowy

- rose-cheeked
- nutty
- prickly
- up a gum tree

Do you know what these things are?

- a beanfeast
- a bean-bag
- thistledown
- a tree-house
- leaf mould
- a fruit machine
- a daisy chain
- rose-coloured spectacles
- a thorny problem

Notes for parents and teachers

Read through this book with children, so that they become familiar with the ideas and words to do with plants. Then try the activities suggested below, to reinforce some of the ideas and give the children further talking points.

Collecting seeds

Make a labelled collection of seeds to compare their shape, size, colour and texture. Wash and keep seeds from fruits such as apples, oranges, avocado pears and peaches. Raid your food cupboard for edible seeds such as rice grains, dried peas, beans, popcorn, sunflower seeds and others. Spread out some hamster or bird food to see what seeds they contain. Collect fruits and seeds from garden plants, such as lupins, dandelions and poppies. In the autumn, search for acorns, sycamore wings, conkers and pine cones.

Good enough to eat

Lay out a variety of different vegetables and help children identify which parts of a plant these are. An interesting selection might include lettuce or spinach leaves, a root vegetable, such as a carrot, turnip or parsnip, celery stalks, pea pods, tomatoes and onions.

What grows?

Try planting bird seed and some frozen peas. Scrape the mud from your boots into some compost. Does anything grow?

Planting experiments

Soak some peas or broad beans for 24 hours and use them to try out a few experiments. Seeds vary, and some will grow better than others. Always use more than one seed in any experiment.

- Does it matter which way I plant a bean?
  Try planting three beans the right way up, three upside-down and three horizontally.

- What happens when I cut a bean in half?
  Plant three whole beans in one pot and three half beans in another pot.

- Do beans need water?
  Plant three beans in one pot and three in another. Regularly water only one of the pots.

- Do beans need light?
  Plant three beans in one pot and three in another. Keep one pot in a cupboard.

- Does the soil type matter?
  Sow three seeds in pots with different types of soil, such as sand, clay, compost, a mixture of sand and soil, and garden soil. Talk about why their growth might be different.

Plant scrapbook

Cut out pictures from brochures and magazines that show plants growing in different climates and environments and make a plant scrapbook. Talk about the reasons for why different kinds of plants grow in different places.

29

Index

Titles in the series

ISBN 1 84138 184 5 (hb)
ISBN 1 84138 377 5 (pb)
ISBN 1 84138 375 9 (big book)

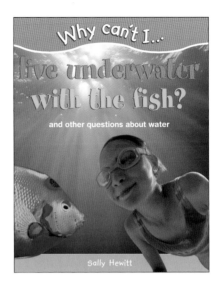

ISBN 1 84138 187 X (hb)
ISBN 1 84138 378 3 (pb)
ISBN 1 84138 376 7 (big book)

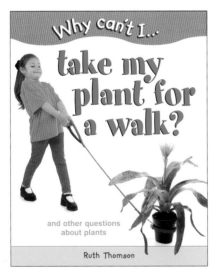

ISBN 1 84138 186 1 (hb)
ISBN 1 84138 741 X (pb)

ISBN 1 84138 185 3 (hb)
ISBN 1 84138 740 1 (pb)